Mystic Aspects Of The Holy Grail Legend

Arthur Edward Waite

Kessinger Publishing's Rare Reprints

Thousands of Scarce and Hard-to-Find Books on These and other Subjects!

- Americana
- Ancient Mysteries
- Animals
- Anthropology
- Architecture
- Arts
- Astrology
- Bibliographies
- Biographies & Memoirs
- Body, Mind & Spirit
- Business & Investing
- Children & Young Adult
- Collectibles
- Comparative Religions
- Crafts & Hobbies
- Earth Sciences
- Education
- Ephemera
- Fiction
- Folklore
- Geography
- Health & Diet
- History
- Hobbies & Leisure
- Humor
- Illustrated Books
- Language & Culture
- Law
- Life Sciences
- Literature
- Medicine & Pharmacy
- Metaphysical
- Music
- Mystery & Crime
- Mythology
- Natural History
- Outdoor & Nature
- Philosophy
- Poetry
- Political Science
- Science
- Psychiatry & Psychology
- Reference
- Religion & Spiritualism
- Rhetoric
- Sacred Books
- Science Fiction
- Science & Technology
- Self-Help
- Social Sciences
- Symbolism
- Theatre & Drama
- Theology
- Travel & Explorations
- War & Military
- Women
- Yoga
- *Plus Much More!*

We kindly invite you to view our catalog list at:
http://www.kessinger.net

THIS ARTICLE WAS EXTRACTED FROM THE BOOK:

Hidden Church of the Holy Graal

BY THIS AUTHOR:

Arthur Edward Waite

ISBN 0766126897

READ MORE ABOUT THE BOOK AT OUR WEB SITE:

http://www.kessinger.net

OR ORDER THE COMPLETE
BOOK FROM YOUR FAVORITE STORE

ISBN 0766126897

Because this article has been extracted from a parent book, it may have non-pertinent text at the beginning or end of it.

Any blank pages following the article are necessary for our book production requirements. The article herein is complete.

BOOK VIII

MYSTIC ASPECTS OF THE GRAAL LEGEND

THE ARGUMENT

I. THE INTRODUCTORY WORDS.—*The Quest of the Holy Graal considered as a religious experiment—Counsels of Perfection in the Quest—Of poverty, obedience and virginity—Of partial success in their absence—Peculiarities in the election of Galahad—The state of sanctity—The descent of Grace—Perpetuity of conditions for the experiment—Further as regards virginity in respect of the Quest—The mystical idea of union—The term of the Quest—Separation of transubstantiation marvels from the final vision of the Graal—The experience of Nasciens—Collateral experience of the Mystics—After what manner grace manifested through the Eucharist—Of a gate of knowledge in the Eucharist—Declaration of the Graal in its mystic aspects.* II. THE POSITION OF THE LITERATURE DEFINED.—*A distinction concerning the literature—Of allegory in the Great Quest—A particular form of development in the Graal Legend—The Graal and the Official Church—The case concerning that Church—The implicits of the literature as elements of the mystic aspects—The Recession of the Graal—How this symbol was perpetuated from the beginning—A light from the Quest of Guiot—Meaning of the Stone in the Crown of Lucifer—The Graal and Eucharistic Wisdom.* III. CONCERNING THE GREAT EXPERIMENT.—*The wonder of all sacredness as the term of Quest—An analogy from Ruysbroeck—Term of the Experiment—External places of the Quest—Of helpers therein*

The Hidden Church of the Holy Graal

—*Of Secret Orders—Communication of Divine Substance—The Channel of the Eucharist—Of Integration in Secret Knowledge—The Office of the Quests—Of Popular Devotions in the Church and of such Fatalities—Our Inheritance from the Past—The open Secret of Tradition—Of things that stand in the way in respect of Christian Mysticism—Latin Christianity—The true way of Experience—An eirenicon in doctrine.* IV. THE MYSTERY OF INITIATION.—*Of the Graal in its correspondence with instituted Mysteries—The mind of scholarship on this subject—Analogies from the literary history of Kabalism and Alchemy—The sacramental message of the Graal—Points of comparison between Graal literature and other cycles of books—A distinction on the question of Initiation—The Hidden Knowledge—An illustration from Masonry—Of a certain leaven working in the texts of the Graal—Testimony to the existence of the Great Experiment—The failure of the external world—A caution in respect of interpretation—The indubitable subsurface sense of Graal books.* V. THE MYSTERY OF FAITH.—*A first summary of the whole subject—The Graal Mystery as a declared pageant of the Eucharist—Its distinctions from the official Sacrament—A profound symbolism—Of secret memorials—The Five Changes of the Graal—Of what remains over from the findings of scholarship—The Church teaching on the Eucharist—Limitations of Graal books—And of books of the Mystics.* VI. THE LOST BOOK OF THE GRAAL.—*Suggestion concerning a concealed Liturgy or Mass-Book—Superfluity of this hypothesis in respect of the present interpretation—General testimony of the literature to a primordial text—The schedule thereof—Whether the evidences are applicable to one book—The results obtained therefrom—Conclusion that the literature could not have arisen from a single prototype—Of admitted*

The Argument

and indisputable prototypes—The alleged Latin source—Southey's opinion—Statement of the Comte de Tressan—Middle ground occupied by Paulin Paris—A lesson from the literature of Alchemy—Of all which remains after abandoning the hypothesis of a single prototype in the ordinary sense—Further concerning the implicits and strange rumours present in Graal literature—Proof that these were not inventions of romance—Hypothesis of a Sanctum Graal *which contained these elements—The negative view of its content—The positive view—The book not seen by those who wrote the romances—The presumable custodians thereof—The rumours thereof—How their prevalence does not involve the existence of any book.*
VII. THE DECLARED MYSTERY OF QUEST.—*Exotics of the whole subject—Of faith and experience—Errors of the Mystic Quest—The Open Door—The Gates and their Wardens—A condition of progress in the Quest—The declared and the hidden knowledge—Suddenness of the Graal Wonders—*Obiter Dicta*—The expression of the whole Quest after a new manner.*

BOOK VIII

MYSTIC ASPECTS OF THE GRAAL LEGEND

I

THE INTRODUCTORY WORDS

SEEING therefore that we have not found in the Celtic Church anything which suffices to explain the chief implicits of the literature and that the watchwords call us forward, there remains another method of research, and of this I will now proceed to make trial. I suppose that there is no need to exhibit in formal words after what manner the Quest of the Holy Graal became in the later texts a religious experiment, and thus justified the titles from which it began in that story of Robert de Borron which is the earliest extant history. Any one who has proceeded so far in the present inquisition as to have reached these lines—even if he is wholly unfamiliar with the old treasury of books—will be aware that the Quest was ruled throughout by the counsels of perfection. These ruled in fact so strongly as to have reached that stage when two of them were implied only—that is, they were taken for granted: (*a*) Voluntary poverty, for the knights possessed nothing, and whatever came into their hands was distributed there and then; (*b*) entire obedience, in dedication to the proposed term, and all the ships of the world burnt with fire behind them; when change came there followed complete *avortement*, as that of Gawain in the Great Quest; (*c*) perpetual chastity, as the only counsel which stands declared—and in this connection it will be remembered that Bors returned to Logres. The zeal of these counsels does not appear—as I have said—to guarantee election utterly: it is rather the test of merit. And I have said also that there may be a certain success without their fulfilment in the absolute degree. In the *Longer Prose Perceval* Gawain received signal favours, yet it is admitted that he was wanting in purity, and hence he could make no response when the questionable mystery appeared once in his presence. The King also beheld the arch-natural Eucharist on the manifested side thereof: but Perceval alone possessed the plenary qualifications in this text. On the other hand, in the story of stories there was one who surpassed him, but not so utterly that they were otherwise than classed together as companions of the Quest. The distinction seems to have been that Galahad dissolved temptation, as one more than human. Perceval carried within him the latent desires of the body, and after beholding the Graal he required the purgation of a hermit's life before he entered into the true inheritance of those thrones which are above. By some of my fellowship in research it has been said most truly, though they do not understand Galahad, that the *haut prince* was just as fit for the Quest at its beginning as he was at its end. Now, that is exactly the sign of perfect vocation—of election as well as calling; the criterion of those who are meant for heaven is that they might ascend thither at any moment. Another test of Galahad was that he knew really from the beginning the whole mystery by the tradition thereof.

I am enumerating here the general implicits of the subject which should be latent in the minds of those whom I address; they do not constitute a question put forward for sifting with a view to a settlement, but of fitness and power to see—of the *verus certusque intuitus animi*, in some degree and proportion. This being passed by those who can suffer the ruling, it

Mystic Aspects of the Graal Legend

will be obvious that the religious experiment about which I begin to speak can depend only from two considerations: (1) the attainment of the sanctified state in the Questing Knights, and (2) the descent of a peculiar Grace upon them. I enumerate both points, though it is obvious that one of them has in another form but now passed through review, but in dealing with a very difficult subject it is necessary to look at it in more than a single light, and I wish to make it clear that the specifics of the sanctified state—by which I mean the counsels of perfection—are not things that are determined in the given case by a trend of thought and emotion at the given period, and are not therefore to be dismissed as a presentation of the ascetic life or as the definition of canons which have now passed into desuetude. The same experiment always demands the same conditions for its success, and to set aside these is really to renounce that, or in this instance it is to reject the experiment as one of the old ecstasies which never came to a term. On the contrary, the experiment of sanctity is always approximating to a term, and the measure of success is the measure of zeal in its pursuit. I propose therefore to look a little closer at one of the counsels of perfection. The essential point regarding the condition of *virgo intacta*—not in respect of the simple physical fact, which has no inherent sanctity, but in respect of its conscious acceptance at what cost soever—is that there neither was nor can be a more perfect symbol of the prepared matter of the work. It is the analogy in utter transcendence of that old adage: *Mens sana in corpore sano*, and its nearest expression is: *Anima immaculata in corpore dedicato, ex hoc nunc et usque*, &c. In other words, the banns of marriage in the higher degrees cannot be proclaimed till the contracting parties are warranted in their respective orders to have that proportion and likeness apart from which no union could be effected. The consummated grade of sanctity is an intimate state of union, and the nearest analogy thereto is found in human marriage; as the latter presupposes in the sacramental order an antecedent or nominal purity, and has for its object the consecration of intercourse which in its absence is of the animal kind, so the antecedent condition in sanctity—or the life of perfect dedication—is in correspondence with the state of *virgo intacta*. I need not say that because these things are analogical so the discourse concerning them partakes of the language of symbolism or that the state itself is a spiritual state. Entire obedience involves no earthly master; voluntary poverty is of all possibility in a palace, and the law would not deny it at the headquarters of an American Trust; as regards chastity, that is guaranteed to those who receive the sacrament of marriage worthily, and it is to be noted that this sacrament differs from baptism, which is administered once and for all, while marriage, in the effects thereof, is administered in continuity as an abiding presence and a grace abounding daily so long as its covenants are observed. On the other hand, the perpetuity of spiritual chastity in the life within does not mean of necessity that man or woman has never known flesh in the physical order. Galahad in the story had the outward signs as well as the inward grace. His Quest was an allegory throughout and sometimes the allegorical motive obtrudes into the expressed matter, which is an error of art.

The term which is proposed in the Quest, as the consideration thereof, will be best given in the words of the Quest itself. "Now at the yeres ende and the self daye after Galahad had borne the croune of gold, he arose up erly and his felawes, and came to the palais, and sawe to fore hem the holy vessel, and a man knelynge on his knees in lykenes of a Bisshop that had aboute hym a grete felaushyp of Angels as it had ben Jhesu Cryst hym self, & thenne he arose and beganne a masse of oure lady. And whan he cam to the sacrament of the masse, and had done, anone he called Galahad and sayd to hym

Mystic Aspects of the Graal Legend

come forthe the servaunt of Jhesu Cryst and thou shalt see that thou hast moche desyred to see, & thenne he began to tremble ryght hard, when the dedely flesshe beganne to beholde the spyrytuel thynges. Thenne he held vp his handes toward heuen, and sayd lord I thanke the, for now I see that that hath ben my desyre many a daye. Now blessyd lord wold I not lenger lyue yf it myghte please the lord, & there with the good man tooke our lordes body betwixe hys handes, and profered it to Galahad, and he receyued hit ryghte gladly and mekely. . . . And there with he kneled doune to fore the table, and made his prayers, and thenne sodenly his soule departed to Jhesu Crist and a grete multitude of Angels bare his soule vp to heuen," &c. In this citation the most important point for our purpose at the living moment rests neither in that which it expresses nor in that which it conceals: it is assumed and realised that such a term is always hidden because it always exceeds expression, and is the closer veiled wherein it is announced the most. But here was the consummation of all, and here was that more open seeing than was granted at Corbenic wherein all the outward offices of things archnatural were set aside utterly. Herein therefore was no vision of transubstantiation changes, and as evidence that this was of concert and not of chance, I have the same report to make concerning the *Longer Prose Perceval;* when the questing knight comes to his own therein no signs and wonders are connected with the Holy Graal. As regards the vision itself, we may remember the words of Nasciens when he attempted to penetrate the secrets within the new Ark of the Covenant. "*Et Nasciens dist que il l'en descouverroit tant comme nule mortieus langue em porroit descouvrir, ne deveroit. Je ai, dist-il veut la coumenchaille dou grant hardiment, l'ocoison des grans savoirs, le fondement des grans religions, le dessevrement des grans félonnies, la démoustranche des grans mierveilles, la mervelle de totes les altrez mervelles, la fin des bontés et des gentillèces vraies.*" This extract from the *Book of the Holy Graal* is thus rendered in the halting measures of Lovelich:

> "'I have sein,' quod the sire Nasciens,
> 'Of alle manere of wykkednesse the defens;
> Of alle boldnesse I have sene the begynneng,
> Of all wittes the fowndyng.
> I have sein the begynneng of Religeown
> And of alle bowntes, bothe al & som,
> And the poyntes of alle gentrye,
> And a merveil of alle merveilles certeinlye.'"

Other masters have expressed the same wonder in other terms, which are the same—as, for example: *quædam prælibatio æternæ vitæ, gustus et suavitas spiritualis, mentis in Deum suspensa elevatio*, &c.

The qualifications of Galahad and Perceval in the Great Quest are not therefore things which are the fashion of a period, like some aspects of what is termed the ascetic mind, but they obtain from *Aleph* to *Tau*, through all grades of expression. Those who speak of the ethical superiority of the *Parsifal* are saying that which, in all moderation and tenderness, signifies that they are still learning the elements of true discipline.

I have now dealt with the indispensable warrants of the state, and the mode of the descent of Grace belongs to the same category; it was a manifestation to the spiritual flowers of Christian knighthood through the Eucharist—the form of symbolism made use of for this purpose being that of transubstantiation. I have already set down what I believe to be the Divine Truth on this subject, but here again we must as our research proceeds approach it from various standpoints; and, for the rest, it must be obvious that of all men I at least should have no call imposed on me to speak of the Holy Graal were it not for its connection with the Blessed Sacrament. It is the passage of the putative reliquary into the Chalice of the Eucharist, the progressive exaltation of its cultus and the consequent transfiguration of the Quest which have substituted insensibly a tale of eternity for a mediæval

Mystic Aspects of the Graal Legend

legend of the Precious Blood; in place of the Abbey of Fécamp, we have Corbenic and Mont Salvatch shining in the high distance, and where once there abode only the suggestion of some relative and rather trivial devotion, we have the presence of that great sign behind which there lies the Beginning and the End of all things.

The romance-writers, seeking in their symbolism a reduction to the evidence of the senses, selected and exaggerated the least desirable side of Eucharistic dogma; but we have no occasion to dispute with them on that score, seeing that — for the skilled craftsman — any material will serve in the purposes of the Great Work. The only point which stands out for our consideration is that—following the sense of all doctrine and the testimony of all experience—the gate by which faith presses into realisation is the gate of that Sacrament from which all others depend—of that Sacrament the institution of which was the last act of Christ and the term of His ministry; thereafter He suffered only until He rose in glory. When therefore the makers of the Graal books designed to show after what manner, and under what circumstances, those who were still in flesh could behold the spiritual things and have opened for them that door of understanding which, according to the keepers of the Old Law, was not opened for Moses, they had no choice in the matter, and it is for this reason that they represent the Bread of Life and the Chalice of the Everlasting Testament as being lifted up in the secret places of Logres, even in the *palais esperiteux*.

Hereof are the mystic aspects of the Great Quest, and it seems to follow that the secret temple of the soul was entered by those who dwelt in the world of romance as by those in the world of learning. The adepts of both schools were saying the same thing at the same period, seeing that during the twelfth and thirteenth centuries, which moved and had their being under the wonderful ægis of the scholastic mind, there began to arise over the intellectual horizon of Europe the light of another experience than that of spiritual truth realised intellectually; this was the experience of the mystic life, which opened—shall we say?—with the name of Bonaventura and closed for the period in question with that of Ruysbroeck.

II

THE POSITION OF THE LITERATURE DEFINED

The books of the Holy Graal are either purely of literary, antiquarian and mythological interest, or they are more. If literary, antiquarian and mythological only, they can and should be left to the antiquaries, the critics and the folk-lore societies. But if more it is not improbable antecedently, having regard to the subject, that the excess belongs to the mystics, and to those generally who recognise that the legends of the soul are met with in many places, often unexpectedly enough, and wherever found that they have issues outside that which is understood commonly and critically by the origin of religious belief. The ascetic and mystic element—to repeat the conventional description — outside the considerations which I have put forward, is for those of all importance, and it is otherwise and invariably the only thing that is really vital in legends. The impression which is left upon the mind after the conclusions of the last sub-section is assuredly that the "divine event" is not especially, or not only, that "towards which creation moves," but a term, both here and now, towards which souls can approximate and wherein they can rest at the centre. Over the threshold of the Galahad Quest we pass as if out of worlds of enchantment, worlds of færie, worlds of the mighty Morgan le Fay, into realms of allegory and dual meaning, and then—transcending allegory—into a region more deeply unrealised; so also, after having reflected on the external side of the romances and the preliminary analogies of things that are inward, we pass, as we approach

Mystic Aspects of the Graal Legend

the end of our research, into a world of which nothing but the veils and their emblazonments have been so far declared. No other romances of chivalry exhibit the characteristics which we discern in the perfect and rectified books of the Holy Graal, but if we do not know categorically why romance came to be the vehicle for one expression of man's highest experience, we have reasons —and more than enough—to determine that it was not automatic, not arbitrary, and yet it was not fortuitous; it came about in the nature of things by the successive exaltation of a legend which had the capacity for exaltation into transcendence. The genesis of the story of Galahad is not like the institution of the ritual belonging to the third craft grade in Masonry, which seems without antecedents that are traceable in the elements—actual or symbolical—of the early building guilds. By successive steps the legend of the Graal was built till it reached that height when the hierarchies could begin to come down and the soul of Galahad could go up. It is important for my own purpose to establish this fact, because in that which remains to be said I must guard against the supposition that a conventional secret society or a sect took over the romances, edited them and interpenetrated the texts with mystic elements. That is the kind of hypothesis which occult interests might have manufactured sincerely enough in the old days, and it would have had a certain warrant because there is ample evidence that this is exactly the kind of work which in given cases was performed by the concealed orders. The Graal, as a literature, came into other hands, which worked after their own manner, and worked well.

There is another fact which is not less important because of certain tendencies recognisable in modern criticism. I will mention it only at the moment, that the reader may be put on his guard mentally; there is no single text in the literature which was or could have been put forward as a veiled *pronunciamento* against the reigning Church on the part of any historical sect, heresy,

The Hidden Church of the Holy Graal

or rival orthodoxy. The pure Christianities and the incipient principles of reform took their quack processes into other quarters. The voices which spoke in the books of the Holy Graal as no voices had ever spoken in romance were not putting forward a mystery which was superior specifically to the mysteries preserved by the official Church. They trended in the same direction as the highest inquisitions move, and that invariably. The most intelligent of all the heresies is only the truth of the Church foreshadowed or travestied. The reforms of the Church are only its essential lights variously refracted. Even modern science, outside the true prerogatives of its election as our growing physical providence, is the notification of the things which do not ultimately matter in comparison with the science of the Church, which is that of the laws ruling in the search after the eternal reality. The Graal at its highest is the simulacrum or effigy of the Divine Mystery within the Church. If she, as an institution, has failed so far—and as to the failure within limits there is no question—to accomplish the transmutation of humanity, the explanation is not merely that she has been at work upon gross and refractory elements—though this is true assuredly—but that in the great mystery of her development she has still to enter into the fruition of her higher consciousness. Hereof are the wounds of the Church, and for this reason she has been in sorrow throughout the ages.

So far I have defined, but in one sense only, the position of the literature. It remains to be said that what I have termed from the beginning the major implicits, as they project vaguely and evasively upon the surface, are integral elements of the mystic aspects. But they must be taken here in connection with one feature of the quests which is in no sense implied, because this will concern us in a very important manner in the next book. I refer to the Recession of the Graal. I have no need to remind any one after so many enumerations that the final testimony of all the French Quests

Mystic Aspects of the Graal Legend

is that, in one or another way, the Graal was withdrawn. It is not always by a removal in space; it is not always by assumption to heaven. In the German cycle the Temple was inaccessible from the beginning and the Palladium never travelled, till—once and for all—it was carried in a great procession to the furthest East. Wolfram left it in primeval concealment; but this did not satisfy one of the later poets, who married—as we have seen—the Graal legend to that of Prester John. Now, it might be more easy to attain translation, like St. Paul, than to find that sanctuary in India where, by the assumption, it must be supposed to remain. But having regard to the hidden meaning which seems to lie behind Wolfram's source he was within the measures of his symbolism when he left the Graal at Mont Salvatch, not removing to the East that which in his case did not come therefrom. Albrecht, who tells of the transit, first took the precaution to change the hallowed object. I believe that the testimony to removal was inherent to the whole conception from the beginning, concurrently with the Secret Words, and that the latter were reflected at a later period into the peculiar claim concerning sacerdotal succession. They were all Eucharistic in their nature. The testimony itself is twofold, because, in addition to the withdrawal of the Living Sign, the texts tell us of the House that is emptied of its Hallows; these are in particular the *Longer Prose Perceval* and the *Quest of Galahad*. There is also Manessier's conclusion of the *Conte del Graal*, but no very important inference is to be drawn therefrom. One of our immediate concerns will be to find the analogies of this prevailing conception elsewhere in the world; the present study of Graal mystic aspects is simply preliminary thereto, and the eduction of the significance behind the major implicits. It is at this point curiously that one element of Graal history which has been somehow ascribed to Guiot comes to our assistance, providing an intermediary between the literature of mystical romance and—as we shall learn—the obvious text-books of the secret schools. It opens, I think, strange vistas of intellectual wonder and enchantment. We have heard already that the Stone which is identified with the Graal in Wolfram was at one time a stone in the crown of Lucifer, and seeing that, according to other legends, the thrones left vacant by the fallen angels are reserved for human souls, it becomes intelligible why the Graal was brought to earth and what is signified by the mystic jewel. The Stone in the crown of Lucifer symbolises the great estate from which the archangel fell. It was held by the fathers of the Church that, when still in the delights of Paradise, Lucifer was adorned by all manner of precious stones, understanding mystically of him what in the text of the prophet Ezekiel is said literally of the Prince of Tyre: *In deliciis paradisi Dei fuisti; omnis lapis preciosus operimentum tuum: sardius, topazius, et jaspis, chrysolithus, et onyx, et beryllus, sapphirus, et carbunculus, et smaragdus*—nine kinds of stones, according to Gregory the Great, because of the nine choirs of angels. And Bartolocci, the Cistercian, following all authorities, understands these jewels to signify the knowledge and other ornaments of grace with which Lucifer was adorned in his original state as the *perfecta similitudo Dei*—in other words, the light and splendour of the hidden knowledge. It follows on this interpretation (1) That the Graal Stone in no sense belongs to folk-lore; (2) that it offers in respect of its origin no connection with the idea of physical maintenance, except in the sense that the things which sustain the soul maintain also the body, because the *panis quotidianus* depends from the *panis supersubstantialis*; (3) that the wisdom of the Graal is an Eucharistic wisdom, because the descent of an archnatural Host takes place annually to renew the virtues thereof; (4) that the correspondence of this is, in other versions of the legend, the Host which is consecrated extra-validly by the Secret Words, and so also the cor-

Mystic Aspects of the Graal Legend

respondence of the Stone which comes from heaven is the Cup which goes thereto; but in fine (5) that the jewel in the crown of Lucifer is called also the Morning Star, and thus it is not less than certain that the Graal returns whence it came.

III

CONCERNING THE GREAT EXPERIMENT

If there be any who at this stage should say that the term of the Holy Graal is not the end of the mysteries—which is the Vision that is He—I would not ask him to define the distinction, but the term in either case, for that which must be said of the one is said also of the other, and if he understands the other it is certain that he understands the one. The Quest of the Holy Graal is for the wonder of all sacredness, there where no sinner can be. The provisional manifestation is in the *Longer Prose Perceval* and the full disclosure—not as to what it is but as to what it is about—is in the romance of Galahad. If, after the *haut prince* had given his final message, "Remember of this unstable world," he had been asked what he had seen which led him to exercise his high prerogative and call to be dissolved, he might have answered: *Visi sunt oculi mei salutare suum*, yet he would have said in his heart: "Eye hath not seen." But it has been divined and foretasted by those who have gone before the cohorts of election in the life that is within and have spoken with tongues of fire concerning that which they have seen in the vista. One approximation has told us that it is the eternal intercourse of the Father and the Son wherein we are enveloped lovingly by the Holy Spirit in that love which is eternal. And him who said this the wondering plaudits of an after-age termed the Admirable Ruysbroeck. He knew little Latin and less Greek, and, speaking from his own root, he had not read the authorities; but he had stood upon

The Hidden Church of the Holy Graal

that shore where the waves of the divine sea baptize the pilgrim, or in that undeclared sphere which is *Kether*, the Crown of Kabalism, whence those who can look further discern that there is *Ain Soph Aour*, the Limitless Light. The equivalent hereof is in that which was said by Jesus Christ to the men of the Quest: "My Knyghtes and my seruantes & my true children whiche ben come oute of dedely lyf in to spyrytual lyf I wyl now no longer hyde me from yow, but ye shal see now a parte of my secretes & of my hydde thynges." And in the measure of that time they knew as they were known in full, that is, by participation in, and correspondence with the Divine Knowledge. Meat indeed: it is in that sense that Christ gave to Galahad "the hyghe mete" and "then he receyved his saueour." The monk who wrote this might have exhausted all the language of the schools, but he also knew little Latin and less Greek, if any, so he said only of the communicants: "They thoughte it soo swete that hit was merveillous to telle." And of Galahad he said later: "He receyued hit ryghte gladly and mekely." But yes, and that is fuller and stronger than all the eloquence of the Master of Sentences. It is the voice of Ruysbroeck—but further simplified—saying the same thing: "And he tastes and sees, out of all bounds, after God's own manner, the riches which are in God's own self, in the unity of the living deep, wherein He has fruition of Himself, according to the mode of His uncreated essence."

This is the Great Term of the Great Experiment followed by the Mystic Schools, and here by its own words the Graal legend is expressed in the terms of this Experiment. It has been made, within their several measures, by all churches, sects and religions, for which reason I have said elsewhere that the skilled craftsman does not quarrel with his tools. All materials are possible; the ascent to eternal life can be made by any ladder, assuming that it is fixed in the height; there is no need to go in search of something that is new and

Mystic Aspects of the Graal Legend

strange. And those who can receive this assurance will, I think, understand why it is that the Church of a man's childhood—assuming that it is a Church and not a latitudinarian chapel of ease or a narrow and voided sect—may and perhaps should contain for him the materials of his work, and these he will be able to adapt as an efficient craftsman. There is neither compulsion nor restraint, but the changes in official religion, the too easy transition from one to another kind, taking the sanctuaries as one takes high grades in Masonry, are a note of weakness rather than a pledge of sincerity, or of the true motive which should impel the soul on its quest.

There are, of course, many helpers of that soul on that progress:

> "We, said the day and the night
>   And the law of gravitation;
> And we, said the dark and the light
>   And the stars in their gyration;
> But I, said Justice, moving
>   To the right hand of the Throne;
> And I, said Fate, approving;
>   I make thy cause mine own."

Among these there are certain of the secret orders—those, I mean, which contain the counterparts of the Catholic tradition—and it is necessary to mention them here because of what follows. They offer no royal road, seeing that such roads there are none; but they do in cases shorten some of the preliminaries, by developing the implicits of a man's own consciousness, which is the setting of the prepared postulant on the proper path. There are, of course, some who enter within them having no special call, and these see very little of that which lies behind their official workings, just as there are many who have been born within the Church, as the body of Christ, but have never entered into the life which is communicated from the soul of Christ. They remain the children of this world, participating—as we hope—according to their degree, in so much of grace and salvation as is possible at the particular time. There are others who, out of all time, have received a high election, and for them the subject is often—in its undivided entirety—found resident in that state of external religious life in which it has pleased God to call them.

The Secret Doctrine in the religions equally and the schools is that of the communication of Divine Substance. I speak of it as secret in both cases, though it is obvious that in the official church there is no instituted reservation or conscious concealment on any point of doctrine or practice; but the language of the heights is not the language of the plains, and that which is heard in the nooks, byways and corners, among brakes and thickets, is not the voice of the rushing waters and the open sea. That is true of it in the uttermost which was said long ago by Paracelsus: *Nihil tam occultum erit quod non revelabitur;* but as there are few with ears to hear, it remains a voice in the wilderness crying in the unknown tongue. We know only that, according to high theology, the Divine Substance is communicated in the Eucharist—normally in the symbolical manner, but, in cases, essentially and vitally according to the true testimonies. It is therefore as if the elements were at times consecrated normally and at times by other words, more secret and efficient archnaturally. Then the enchantments terminate which are the swoon of the sensitive life in respect of the individual, who enters into real knowledge—the soul's knowledge before that supervened which is termed mystically the fall into matter. The Great Experiment is therefore one of reintegration in the secret knowledge before the Fall, and when, or if, the Holy Graal is identified with the stone in the crown of Lucifer, that which is indicated thereby is (*a*) the perpetuation of this secret knowledge, and (*b*) that under all circumstances there is a way back whence we came. So close also those times of adventure which—among other things and manifold—are the life of external activity governed by the spirit of the world, and this is accomplished by taking the great secret into the heart of the heart, as if the Blessed Sacrament, truly and virtually, into the inmost being.

Of such is the office of the Quests, but it is understood that it is not of my concern to enumerate these particulars as present consciously in the minds of the old monastic *scriptores*, who wrote the greatest of the books; they spoke of the things which they knew; without reference or intention they said what others had said of the same mysteries, and the testimony continued through the centuries. The story of the assumption of Galahad draws into romance the hypothesis of the Catholic Church concerning the term of all sanctity manifested; in both it is attained through the Eucharist. I mean to say that this is, by the hypothesis, the normal channel of the Divine Favour, and the devotion which was shown by the saints to the Sacrament of the Altar was not like the particular, sentimental disposition in minds of piety to the Precious Blood or the Heart of Jesus. Concerning these exercises I have no call to pronounce, but among the misjudgments on spiritual life in the Roman communion has been the frittering of spiritual powers in the popular devotion. If the Great Mysteries of the Church are insufficient to command the dedication of the whole world, then the world is left best under interdict, just as no pictures at all are better than those which are bad in art, and no books than those which are poor and trivial.

There is one point more, because here we have been trending in directions which will call for more full consideration presently. I have mentioned Secret Orders, and I cannot recall too early that any Secret Tradition—either in the East or the West—has been always an open secret in respect of the root-principles concerning the Way, the Truth and the Life. We are only beginning, and that by very slow stages, to enter into our inheritance from the past; and still perhaps in respect of the larger part we are seeking far and wide for the mystic treasures of Basra. It is therefore desirable to remember that the great subjects of preoccupation are all at our very doors.

One reason, of which we shall hear again in another connection, is because among the wise of the ages, in whatsoever regions of the world, I do not think that there has been ever any difference of opinion about the true object of research; the modes and form of the Quest have varied, and that widely, but to a single point have all the ways converged. Therein is no change or shadow of vicissitude. We may hear of shorter roads, and we might say at first sight that such a suggestion must be true indubitably; but in one sense it is rather a convention of language and in another it is a commonplace which tends to confuse the issues. It is a convention of language, because the Great Quests are not pursued in time or place, and it would be just as true to say that in a journey from the circumference to the centre all roads are the same length, supposing that they are straight roads. It is a commonplace, because if any one should enter the byways, or return on his path and restart, it is obvious that he must look to be delayed. Furthermore, it may be true that all paths lead ultimately to the centre, and that if we descend into hell there may be still a way back to the light: yet in any house of right reason the issues are too clear to consider such extrinsic possibilities.

On this and on any consideration, we have to lay down one irrevocable law—that he who has resolved—setting all things else aside—to enter the path of the Quest must look for his progress in proportion as he pursues holiness for its own sake. He who in the Secret Orders dreams of the adeptship which they claim, *ex hypothesi*, to impart to those who can receive, and who does not say sanctity in his heart till his lips are cleansed, and then does not say it with his lips, is not so much far from the goal as without having conceived regarding it.

Now, it is precisely this word sanctity which takes us back, a little unintentionally, to the claim of the Church, and raises the question whether we are to interpret it according to the mind of the Church or another mind. My answer is that I doubt if the Great Experiment was

Mystic Aspects of the Graal Legend

ever pursued to its term in Christian times on the part of any person who had once been incorporated by the mystical body but subsequently had set himself aside therefrom. When the Quest of the Holy Graal was in fine achieved, there were some who, as we know, were translated, but others became monks and hermits; they were incorporated, that is to say, by the official annals of sanctity. I am dealing here with what I regard as a question of fact, not with antecedent grounds, and the fact is that the Church has the Eucharist. It may in certain respects have hampered Christian Mysticism by the restriction of its own consciousness so especially to the literal side; it may, on the historical side, have approached too often that picture of a certain King of Castle Mortal, who sold God for money; it may in this sense have told the wrong story, though the elements placed in its hands were the right and true elements. But not only is it certain that because of these elements we have to cleave as we can to the Church, but—speaking as a *doctor dubitantium*—I know that the Church Mystic on the highest throne of its consciousness does not differ in anything otherwise than *per accidentia*—or alternatively, the prudence of expression—from formal Catholic doctrine. It can say with its heart of knowledge what the ordinary churchman says with his lips of faith; the *Symbolum* remains; it has not taken on another meaning; it has only unfolded itself, like a flower, from within. The Christian Mystic can therefore recite his *Credo in unum Deum* by clause and by clause, including *in unam sanctam catholicam et apostolicam ecclesiam*, and there is neither heresy in the construction nor Jesuitry in the *arrière pensée*. Above all, the path of the mystic does not pass through the heresies. It has seemed worth while to make this plain, because the Holy Graal is the Catholic Quest drawn into romance.

IV

THE MYSTERY OF INITIATION

The Mystic Aspects of the Graal legend having been developed up to this stage, the question arises whether they have points of correspondence with any scheme of the Instituted Mysteries, whether any element which is present in the romances can be regarded as a faint and far off reflection of something which at that time was known and done in any secret schools. The possibility has presented itself already to the mind of scholarship, which, having performed admirable work in the study of the Graal texts, is still in search of a final explanation concerning them. The shadow of the old Order of the Temple has haunted them in dreams fitfully, and they have lingered almost longingly over vague imagined reflections of the Orgies of Adonis and Tammuz. As behind the Christian symbolism of the extant literature there spreads the whole world of pagan folk-lore, so—at least antecedently—there might be implied also some old scheme of the epopts. It seems permissible therefore to offer an alternative, under proper judgments of reserve, as something which—if otherwise considerable—may be held tentatively until later circumstances of research either lead it into demonstration or furnish a fitting substitute. The Graal legends are comparable to certain distinct literatures with which the theory here put forward will connect them by a twofold consanguinity of purpose. Scholarship had scarcely troubled itself with the great books of Kabalism till it was found or conceived that they could be made to enforce the official doctrines of Christianity. Many errors of enthusiasm followed, but the books of the mystery of Israel became in this manner the public heritage of philosophy, and we are now able to say after what manner it enters into the general scheme of mystic knowledge. The

Mystic Aspects of the Graal Legend

literature of alchemy, in like manner, so long as it was in the hands of certain amateurs of infant science and its counterfeits, remained particular to themselves, and outside a questionable research in physics it had no office or horizon until it was discovered or inferred that many curious texts of the subject had been written in a language of subterfuge, that in place of a metallurgical interest it was concerned in its way with the keeping of spiritual mysteries. There were again errors of enthusiasm, but a corner of the veil was lifted. Now, it is indubitably the message of the Graal that there is more in the Eucharist than is indicated by the sufficing graces imparted to the ordinary communicant, and if it is possible to show that behind this undeclared excess there lies that which has been at all times sought by the Wise, that *est in sacramento quicquid quærunt sapientes*, then the Graal literature will enter after a new manner into our heritage from the past, and another corner of the veil will be lifted on the path of knowledge. It will be seen that the literature—contrary to what it appears on the surface—is not without points of comparison in other Christian cycles—that it does not stand exactly alone, even if its consanguinities, though declared by official religion, are not entirely before the face of the world but within the sanctuaries of secret fraternities. To suggest this is not to say that these stories of old are a defined part or abstract of any mysteries of initiation; they are at most a byway winding through a secret woodland to a postern giving upon the chancel of some great and primeval abbey.

Those who have concerned themselves with the subject of hidden knowledge will know that the secret claims have been put forth under all manners of guises. This has arisen to some extent naturally enough in the course of the ages and under the special atmosphere of motives peculiar to different nations. It has also come about through the institution of multiples of convention on the part of some who have become in later times the custodians of the mysteries, such wardens having been actuated by a twofold purpose, firstly, to preserve their witness in the world, and, secondly, to see that the knowledge was, as far as might be, kept away from the world. This is equivalent to saying that the paramount law of silence has of necessity a permanent competitor in the law of the sign. We may take the readiest illustration in the rituals of Craft Masonry. They contain the whole marrow of *bourgeoisie*, but they contain also the shadow of the great mysteries revealed occasionally. The unknown person or assembly which conceived the closing of the Lodge according to one of the grades had a set of moral feelings in common with those of all the retired masters in the craft of joinery, and a language like a journeyman carpenter, but this notwithstanding the words of the adepts had passed over them and they spoke of the Hidden Token as no one had ever spoken before. That closing gives the true explanation of the secret which cannot be told and yet is imparted quite simply; of that mystery which has never been expressed and can yet be recited by the least literate occupant of the chair placed in Wisdom. Nor does it prove in communication to be anything that is strictly unfamiliar. And yet the explanation, so far from making the concealed part of the rite familiar and a thing of no moment, has built about the concealment a wall of preservation which has made its real significance more profound and in the minds of the adepts more important.

The Graal literature is open to a parallel criticism, and the result is also the same. Whatever disappointment may await, in fine, the pursuit of an inquiry like the present, partly on account of the uncouth presentation of important symbolism to the mind of the early romancist, partly by reason of the inherent defect of romance as a vehicle of symbolism, and more than either by the fatal hiatus brought about through the loss of the earliest documents, there is enough evidence to show that a very strange leaven was working in the mass of the texts. Let me add in respect of it, with all necessary reservations and in no illiberal spirit, that the quality of this leaven can be appreciated scarcely by those who are unacquainted (*a*) with the inward phases of the life of Christian sanctity during the Middle Ages, after which period the voices sound uncertain and the consciousness of experience more remote, and (*b*) with the interior working of those concealed orders of which the Masonic experiment is a part only, and elementary at that. The most important lights are therefore either in the very old books or in the catholic motive which characterises secret rituals that, whether old or not, have never entered into the knowledge of the outside world.

The testimony is of two kinds invariably—first of all, to the existence of the Great Experiment and the success with which, under given circumstances, it can be carried to its term, and, secondly, to a great failure in respect of the external world. The one is reflected by the achieved Quest of the Holy Graal, and the other by the removal of the Graal. In respect of the one it is as if a great mystery had been communicated at one time in the external places, but as if the communication had afterwards been suspended, the secret had as if died. In respect of the other, it is as if the House of Doctrine had been voided. Did these statements exhaust the content of the alternatives, the testimony might be that of a sect, but we shall see at the proper time after what manner they conform to external doctrine, even if the keepers of that doctrine should themselves be unable to see the law of the union.

The great literatures and the great individual books may be often at this day as so many counters or heaps of letters put into the hands of the mystic, and he interprets them after his own manner, imparting to them that light which, at least intellectually, abides in himself. I make this formal statement because I realise that it is perilous for my position and because it enables me to add that though literatures may be clay in our hands, we must not suppose that they who in the first place put a shape of their own kind on the material which they had ingarnered were invariably conscious that it would bear that other seal and impression which we set upon it in our own minds as the one thing that is desirable. It is too much to suppose that behind the external sense of texts there was always designed that inward and illusory significance which in some of them we seem to trace so indubitably. The Baron de la Motte Fouqué once wrote a beautiful and knightly romance in which a correspondent discovered a subtle and complete allegory, and the author, who planned, when he wrote it, no subsurface meaning, did not less sincerely confess to the additional sense, explaining in reply that high art in literature is true upon all the planes. There are certain romances which are found to connect in this manner with the mystery of our science—that is to say, in the non-intentional way, and we must only be thankful to discern that there is the deep below the deep, without pressing interpenetration into a formal scheme. It is well to notice this position and thus go before a criticism which presents itself rather than calls to be sought out. The books of the Holy Graal are not exactly of this kind. A text which says that certain secret words were once imparted under very wonderful and exceptional circumstances is certainly obtruding a meaning behind meaning; another which affirms that a certain mythical personage was ordained secretly, owing to a similar intervention, and was made thereby the first Bishop of Christendom, manifests an ulterior motive, or there are no such motives in the world. And further, when the two great Quests of the whole literature are written partly in the form of confessed allegory, it is not unreasonable to infer that they had some such motive throughout; while, in fine, as their express, undisguised intention is to show the existence of an arch-natural Mass, the graces and the mysteries of which can be experienced and seen by some who are of

Mystic Aspects of the Graal Legend

perfect life, then the interpretation which illustrates this intention by the mystic side of Eucharistic doctrine in the Church offers a true construction, and its valid criticism is *vere dignum et justum est, æquum et salutare.* I will pour three cups to the health and coronation of him who shall discover the speculative proto-Perceval of primeval folk-lore, yet on the present subject let him and all other brethren in the holy places of research keep silence, unless God graces them with agreement. The unknown writers of the *Longer Prose Perceval* and the *Quest of Galahad* spoke of the Great Experiment as those who knew something of their theme and bore true witness on the term of the research.

We know in our own hearts that eternity is the sole thing which signifies ultimately and great literature should confess to no narrower horizon. It happens that they begin sometimes by proposing a lesser theme, but they are afterwards exalted; and this was the case with the Graal books, which were given the early legends of Perceval according to the office of Nature, but afterwards the legend of Galahad according to the Law of Grace.

V

THE MYSTERY OF FAITH

We have now reached a certain definite stage in the high debate and can institute a preliminary summary of the whole subject. It is known that the mystery of faith in Christianity is above all things the Eucharist, in virtue of which the Divine Master is ever present in his Church and is always communicated to the soul; but having regard to the interdictions of our age-long exile we receive only a substituted participation in the life of the union. The Graal mystery is the declared pageant of the Eucharist, which, in virtue of certain powers set forth under the veil of consecrating words, is in some way, not indeed a higher mystery than that of the external church, but its demonstration in the transcendant mode. We have only to remember a few passages in the *Book of the Holy Graal*, in the *Longer Prose Perceval*, and in the *Quest of Galahad* to understand the imputed distinction as: (*a*) The communication in the Eucharist of the whole knowledge of the universe from Aleph to Tau; (*b*) the communication of the Living Christ in the dissolution of the veils of Bread and Wine; (*c*) the communication of the secret process by which the soul passes under divine guidance from the offices of this world to heaven, the keynote being that the soul is taken when it asks into the great transcendence. This is the implied question of the Galahad legend as distinguished from the Perceval question. There are those who are called but not chosen at all, like Gawain. There are those who get near to the great mystery but have not given up all things for it, and of these is Lancelot. There is the great cohort, like the apocalyptic multitude which no man can number—called, elected and redeemed in the lesser ways, by the offices of the external Church—and of these is the great chivalry of the Round Table. There are those who go up into the Mountain of the Lord and return again, like Bors; they have received the last degrees, but their office is in this world. In fine, there are those who follow at a long distance in the steep path, and of these is the transmuted Perceval of the Galahad legend. It is in this sense that, exalted above all and more than all things rarefied into a great and high quintessence, the history of the Holy Graal becomes the soul's history, moving through a profound symbolism of inward being, wherein we follow as we can, but the vistas are prolonged for ever, and it well seems that there is neither a beginning to the story nor a descried ending.

We find also the shadows and tokens of secret memorials which have not been declared in the external, and by the strange things which are hinted, we seem to see that the temple of the Graal on Mont Salvatch is

Mystic Aspects of the Graal Legend

not otherwise than as the three tabernacles which it was proposed to build on Mount Tabor. Among indications of this kind there are two only that I can mention. As in the prologue to the *Book of the Holy Graal*, we have heard that the anonymous but not unknown hermit met on a memorable occasion with one who recognised him by certain signs which he carried, giving thus the unmistakable token of some instituted mystery in which both shared: as in the *Longer Prose Perceval* we have seen that there is an account of five changes in the Graal which took place at the altar, being five transfigurations, the last of which assumed the seeming of a chalice, but at the same time, instead of a chalice, was some undeclared mystery: so the general as well as the particular elements of the legend in its highest form offer a mystery the nature of which is recognised by the mystic through certain signs which it carries on its person; yet it is declared in part only and what remains, which is the greater part, is not more than suggested. It is that, I believe, which was seen by the maimed King when he looked into the Sacred Cup and beheld the secret of all things, the beginning even and the end. In this sense the five changes of the Graal are analogous to the five natures of man, as these in their turn correspond to the four aspects of the Cosmos and that which rules all things within and from without the Cosmos. I conclude therefore that the antecedents of the Cup Legend are (1) *Calix meus quam inebrians est*; (2) the Cup which does not pass away; (3) the *vas insigne electionis*. The antecedent of the Graal question is: Ask, and ye shall receive. The antecedent of the Enchantment of Britain is the swoon of the sensitive life, and that of the adventurous times is: I bring not peace, but a sword; I come to cast fire upon the earth, and what will I but that it should be enkindled? The closing of these times is taken when the Epopt turns at the altar, saying *Pax Dei tecum*. But this is the peace which passes understanding and it supervenes upon the *Mors osculi*—the mystic

The Hidden Church of the Holy Graal

Thomas Vaughan's "death of the kiss"—after which it is exclaimed truly: "Blessed are the dead which die in the Lord from henceforth and for ever." It follows therefore that the formula of the Supernatural Graal is: *Panem cœlestem accipiam;* that of the Natural Graal, namely, the Feeding Dish, is: *Panem nostrum quotidianum da nobis hodie;* and the middle term: "Man doth not live by bread alone." I should add: These three there are one; but this is in virtue of great and high transmutations. So, after all the offices of scholarship—pursued with that patience which wears out worlds of obstacles—it proves that there is something left over, that this something bears upon its surface the aspects of mystic life, that hereof is our heritage, and that we can enter and take possession because other claimants there are none. The books of the Holy Graal do tell us of a sanctuary within the sanctuary of Christendom, wherein there are reserved great sacraments, high symbols, relics that are of all most holy, and would be so accounted in all the external ways; but of these things we have heard otherwise in certain secret schools. It follows therefore that we as mystics can lift up our eyes because there is a Morning Light which we go to meet with exultation, *portantes manipulos nostros.* We shall find the paths more easy because of our precursors, who have cleared the tangled ways and have set up landmarks and beacons, by which perchance we shall be led more straightly into our own, though in their clearing and surveying they did not at all know that they were working for us.

It is recognised by the Catholic Church that the Eucharist is at this time the necessity of our spiritual life, awaiting that great day when our daily bread shall itself become the Eucharist, no longer that substitute provided in our material toil and under the offices of which we die. The body is communicated to the body that the Spirit may be imparted to the soul. *Spiritus ipse Christi animæ infunditur,* and this is the illustration of ecstasy. But in these days—as I have hinted—it

Mystic Aspects of the Graal Legend

works only through the efficacy of a symbol, and this is why we cannot say in our hearts: *A carne nostro caro Christi ineffabile modo sentitur*, meaning *Anima sponsæ ad plenissimam in Christum transformationem sublimatur*. Hence, whether it is St. John of the Cross speaking of the Ascent of Mount Carmel or Ruysbroeck of the Hidden Stone, the discourse is always addressed to Israel in the wilderness, not in the Land of Promise. Hence also our glass of vision remains clouded, like the sanctuary; and even the books of the mystics subsist under the law of the interdict and are expressed in the language thereof. Those of the Holy Graal are written from very far away in the terms of transubstantiation, presented thaumaturgically under all the veils of grossness, instead of the terms of the *Epiclesis* in the language of those who have been ordained with the holy oils of the Comforter. In other books the metaphysics of the Lover and the Beloved have been rendered in the tongue of the flesh, forgetting that it bears the same relation to the illusory correspondence of human unions that the Bread of the Eucharist bears to material nutriment. The true analogy is in the contradistinction between the elements of bodies and minds. The high analogy in literature is the Supper at the Second Table in the poem of Robert de Borron. That was a spiritual repast, where there was neither eating nor drinking. For this reason the symbolic fish upon the table conveyed to the Warden the title of Rich Fisher, and it is in this sense—that is to say, for the same reason—that the saints become Fishers of Men. We shall re-express the experience of the mystic life in terms that will make all things new when we understand fully what is implied by the secret words: *Co-opertus et absconditus sponsus*.

The Hidden Church of the Holy Graal

VI

THE LOST BOOK OF THE GRAAL

We have seen, in considering the claim of the Celtic Church to recognition as a possible guiding and shaping spirit of the Graal literature, that one speculation regarding it was the existence in concealment of a particular book, a liturgy of some kind, preferably a Book of the Mass. I have no definite concern in the hypothesis, as it is in no sense necessary to the interpretation which I place upon the literature; but the existence of one or more primordial texts is declared so invariably in the romances that, on the surface at least, it seems simpler to presume its existence, and it becomes thus desirable to ascertain what evidence there is otherwise to be gleaned about it. As it has been left so far by scholarship, the question wears almost an inscrutable or at least an inextricable aspect, and its connection with the mystic aspects of the Holy Graal may be perhaps rather adventitious than accidental, but it is introduced here as a preliminary to those yet more abstruse researches which belong to the ninth book.

We must in the first place set aside from our minds the texts which depend from one another, whether the earlier examples are extant or not. The vanished *Quest* of Guiot—priceless as its discovery would be—is not the term of our research. We must detach further those obviously fabulous chronicles by the pretence of which it is supposed that the several quests and histories were perpetuated for the enlightenment of posterity. No one is wondering seriously whether the knightly adventures of the Round Table were reduced into great chronicles by the scribes of King Arthur's court, for which assurance we have the evidence of the *Huth Merlin*—among several deponents. There are other sources which may be equally putative, but it is these which raise the ques-

Mystic Aspects of the Graal Legend

tion, and I proceed to their enumeration as follows: (1) That which contained the greatest secret of the world, a minute volume which would lie in the hollow of a hermit's hand—in a word, the text presupposed by the prologue to the *Book of the Holy Graal;* (2) that which is ascribed to Master Blihis—the *fabulator famosus*—by the *Elucidation* prefixed to the *Conte del Graal;* (3) that which is called the Great Book by Robert de Borron, containing the Great Secret to which the term Graal is referred, a book of many histories, written by many clerks, and by him communicated apparently to his patron, Walter Montbéliard; (4) that which the Count of Flanders gave to Chrétien de Troyes with instructions to retell it, being the best story ever recited in royal court; (5) that which the Hermit Blaise codified with the help of the secret records kept by the Wardens of the Graal; (6) that which the author of the *Longer Prose Perceval* refers to the saintly man whom he calls Josephus; (7) that which the Jew Flegitanis transcribed from the time-immemorial chronicles of the starry heavens.

The palmary problem for our solution is, whether in the last understanding a mystery book or a Mass book, these cryptic texts can be regarded as "seven and yet one, like shadows in a dream"—or rather, as many inventions concerning one document. If we summarise the results which were obtained from them, we can express them by their chief examples thus: (1) From the prototype of the *Book of the Holy Graal* came the super-apostolical succession, the ordination of Joseph II., the dogma of transubstantiation manifested arch-naturally, and the building of Corbenic as a Castle of Perils and Wonders girt about the Holy Graal; (2) from the prototype of the *Elucidation* we have the indicible secret of the Graal, the seven discoveries of its sanctuary, the account of the Rich Fisherman's skill in necromancy and his protean transformations by magical art; (3) from the prototype of Robert de Borron we have the Secret Words, by him or subsequently referred to Eucharistic consecration; (4) from the prototype of Chrétien we have the history of Perceval le Gallois, so far as it was taken by him; (5) from the putative chronicle of Blaise and his scribes, antecedent and concurrent, we have all that which belongs to the history of Merlin, the foundation of the Round Table and the Siege Perilous; (6) from the prototype of the *Longer Prose Perceval* we have Perceval's later history, his great and final achievements—unlike all else in the literature, more sad, more beautiful, more strange than anything told concerning him; (7) from the prototype of Guiot, we have the Graal presented as a stone, and with an ascribed antecedent history which is the antithesis of all other histories. Had I set up these varying versions in the form of seven propositions on the gates of Salerno or Salamanca and offered to maintain their identity in a thesis against all comers, I suppose that I could make out a case with the help of scholastic casuistry and the rest of the dialectical subtleties; but in the absence of all motive, and detached as regards the result, I can only say in all reason that the quests and the histories as we have them never issued from a single quest or a single history. We may believe, if we please, that the book of the Count of Flanders was really the *Quest* of Guiot, reducing the sources to six, and a certain ingenuity —with courage towards precarious positions—may help us to further eliminations, but the root-difficulty will remain—that the Quests, as we have them, exclude one another and so also do some of the histories. It follows that there were many prototypes, or alternatively that there were many inventions in respect of the sources. In respect of the Perceval legends there was the non-Graal folk-lore myth, which accounts for their root-matter but not for their particular renderings and their individual Graal elements; the nearest approximation to these myths and their nearest issue in time may have been the *Quest* of Guiot. One general

Mystic Aspects of the Graal Legend

source of De Borron was transparently the *Evangelium Nicodemi*, complicated by later Joseph legends, including the tradition of Fécamp, but more than all by another source, of which he had heard at a distance and of which I shall speak at the close. The *Quest of Galahad* makes no claim to a prototype, but it reflects extant manuscripts of the Greater Chronicles; for the rest, its own story was all important; it cared nothing for antecedents, and it is only by sporadic precaution, outside its normal lines, that it registers at the close after what manner it pretended to be reduced into writing. The prototypes of this text are in the annals of sanctity, except in so far as it reflects—and it does so indubitably—some rumours which Robert de Borron had drawn into romance. As regards Galahad himself, his romance is a great invention derived from the prose *Lancelot*. The *Longer Prose Perceval* is an invention after another manner; there is nothing to warrant us in attaching any credit to the imputed source in Josephus, but the book drew from many places and transmuted that which it drew with a shaping spirit; it is an important text for those rumours to which I have referred darkly. It works, like the *Quest of Galahad*, in a high region of similitude, and its pretended source is connected intimately with the second Joseph of the Greater Chronicles.

We are now in a position to deal with a further ascription which is so general in the literature and was once rather widely accepted—namely, that of a Latin source. It will be noted that this is a simple debate of language and it leaves the unity or multiplicity of the prototypes an open question. It is worth mentioning, because it enters into the history of the criticism of Graal literature. There is no need to say that it is now passed over by scholarship, and the first person to reject it was Robert Southey in his preface to the edition of Sir Thomas Malory's *Morte d'Arthur* which passes under his name, though he had no hand in the editing of the text itself. "I do not believe," he says, "that any of these romances ever existed in Latin,—by whom, or for whom, could they have been written in that language?" For the romances as romances, for *Meliadus de Leonnois*, *Gyron le Courtois*, and so forth, the question has one answer only, the fact notwithstanding that the prologue to *Gyron* draws all the prose tales of the Round Table from what it terms the Latin *Book of the Holy Graal*. There is one answer also for any version of the Graal legend, as we now know it. Even for that period, the Comte de Tressan committed a serious absurdity when he affirmed that the whole literature of Arthurian chivalry, derived by the Bretons from the ancient and fabulous chronicles of Melkin and Tezelin, was written in Latin by Rusticien de Pise, who was simply a compiler and translator into the Italian tongue and was concerned, as such, chiefly with the Tristram cycle. At the same time it is possible to take too extreme a view. In his preface to another work, *Palmerin of England*, Southey remarks that "every reader of romance knows how commonly they were represented as translations from old manuscripts," and that such an ascription, "instead of proving that a given work was translated, affords some evidence that it is original." The inference is worded too strongly and is scarcely serious as it stands, but the fact itself is certain; and indeed the Graal romances belong to a class of literature which was prone to false explanations in respect both of authorship and language. Still, there is something to be said for the middle ground suggested, now long ago, on the authority of Paulin Paris, that while it is idle to talk of romances in the Latin language, there is nothing impossible in the suggestion that the sacramental legend of Joseph of Arimathæa and his Sacred Vessel may have existed in Latin. From his point of view it was a Gradual, and he even goes so far as to speculate (*a*) that it was preserved at Glastonbury; (*b*) that it was not used by the monks because it involved schism with Rome; and (*c*) that, like the Jew of Toledo's

Mystic Aspects of the Graal Legend

transcript, it was forgotten for three centuries—till it was recalled by the quarrel between Henry II. and the Pope. This is, of course, fantasy, but the bare supposition of such a Latin legend would account in a natural manner for an ascription that is singularly consistent, while it would not pretend to represent the lost imaginary prototypes of the whole complex literature.

In this connection we might do worse than take warning by one lesson from the literature of alchemy. The early writers on this subject were in the habit of citing authorities who, because they could not be identified, were often regarded as mythical; but all the same they existed in manuscript; they might have been found by those who had taken the trouble; and they are now familiar to students by the edition of Berthelot. In matters of this kind we do not know what a day may bring forth, and from all standpoints the existence of a pious legend—orthodox or heretical, Roman or Breton—concerning Joseph and his Hallow would be interesting, as it must also be valuable. Unfortunately, the Quest of the Holy Graal in respect of its missing literature is after the manner of a greater enterprise, for there are many who follow it and few that come to the term of a new discovery. There are authorities now in England to whom the possibility of such a text might not be unacceptable, though criticism dwells rightly upon the fact that there is no mention of the Holy Vessel in the earliest apocryphal records of the evangelisation of Britain by Joseph. We have heard already of one Latin memorial among the archives of Fécamp, but of its date we know nothing, and its conversion legend does not belong to this island.

Having thus determined, as I think, the question of a single prototype accounting for all the literature, we have to realise that everything remains in respect of the mystery of origin—now the wonder element of things unseen and heard of dimly only, sometimes expressed imperfectly in Nature poems, which have no concern therein; now what sounds like a claim on behalf of the Celtic Church; now sacramental legends incorporated by Latin Christianity into the great body of romances. But I speak here of things which are approximate and explicable in an atmosphere of legend married to a definite world of doctrine. There is nothing in these to explain (*a*) the report of a secret sanctuary in all the texts without any exception whatever, for even the foolish *Crown of all Adventures* allocates its house of ghosts to the loneliest of all roads; (*b*) the Secret Words of Consecration; (*c*) the arch-natural Mass celebrated in three of the texts; (*d*) the hidden priesthood; (*e*) the claim to a holy and hidden knowledge; (*f*) the removal of this knowledge from concealment to further concealment, because the world was not worthy. These are the rumours to which I have alluded previously, and I have attached to them this name, because there is nothing more obvious in the whole cycle of literature than the fact that those who wrote of them did not—for the most part—know what they said. Now, it is a canon of reasonable criticism that writers who make use of materials which they do not understand are not the inventors thereof. It had never entered into the heart of Robert de Borron that his Secret Words reduced the ordinary Eucharist to something approaching a semblance; to the putative Walter Map that his first Bishop of Christendom put the whole Christian apostolate into an inferior place; to any one of the romancers that his Secret Sanctuary was the claim of an orthodoxy in transcendence; to the authors in particular of the *Longer Prose Perceval* and the *Quest of Galahad* that their implied House of the Hallows came perilously near to the taking of the heart out of Christendom. So little did these things occur to them that their materials are mismanaged rather seriously in consequence. Had the first Bishop of Christendom ordained those whom he intended to succeed him, I should not bring this charge against the author of that text which presents the consecration of

Mystic Aspects of the Graal Legend

the second Joseph in all its sanctity and wonder. But, as a matter of fact, the custody of the Holy Graal passed into the hands of a layman, and we are offered the picture of a priest anointed by Christ who does not even baptize, a hermit on one occasion being obtained to administer this simplest of all the sacraments. And yet this first bishop of Christendom had ordained many and enthroned some at Sarras. There is a similar crux in the *Lesser Holy Graal* and its companion poem. One would have thought that the possession of the Secret Words would be reserved to those bearing the seal of the priesthood; but it is not suggested that Joseph of Arimathæa was either ordained by Christ or by any bishop of the Church; his successor, Brons, was simply a disciple saved out of rejected Jerusalem; and Perceval, the *tiers hons*, was a knight of King Arthur's court. Of two things, therefore, one: either the makers of romance who brought in these elements knew not what they said, and reflected at a far distance that which they had heard otherwise, or the claims are not that which they appear on the surface; beneath them there is a deeper concealment; there was something behind the Eucharistic aspect of the mysterious formula and something behind the ordination in transcendence; there was in fine a more secret service than that of the Mass. I accept the first alternative, but without prejudice to the second, which is true also, as we shall see later, still on the understanding that what subtended was not in the mind of romance.

If it is necessary or convenient to posit the existence of a single primordial book, then the *Sanctum Graal, Liber Gradalis,* or *Missa de Corpore Christi* contained these elements, and it contained nothing or little of the diverse matter in the literature. It was not a liturgy connected with the veneration of a relic or of certain relics; it did not recite the legend of Joseph or account in what manner soever for the conversion of Britain. It was a Rite of the Order of Melchisedech and it communicated the arch-natural sacrament *ex hypothesi*. The prologue to the *Book of the Holy Graal* has what one would be inclined to call a rumour of this Mass, after which there supervened an ecstasy as a foretaste of the Divine Rapture. The term thereof was the Vision which is He, and the motive of the dilucid experience is evaded—consciously or not, but, I say, in truth unconsciously—by the substitute of reflections upon difficulties concerning the Trinity. No Graal writer had ever seen this book, but the rumour of it was about in the world. It was held in reserve not in a monastery at Glastonbury, but by a secret school of Christians whose position in respect of current orthodoxy was that of the apex to the base of any perfect triangle—its completion and not its destruction. There was more of the rumour abroad than might have been expected antecedently, as if a Church of St. John the Divine were planted somewhere in the West, but not in the open day. There was more of the rumour, and some makers of texts had heard more than others. We know that in the prologue to the *Book of the Holy Graal* there is what might be taken as a reference to this company, the members of which were sealed, so that they could recognise one another by something which they bore upon their persons. When, in the *Quest of Galahad*, the nine strange knights came from the East and the West and the North and the South to sit down, or to kneel rather, at the Table of the Graal, they entered without challenge, they took their proper places and were saluted and welcomed, because they also bore the seal of the secret order. King Pelles went out because he was not on the Quest, because his part was done, because he had attained and seen, for which reason he departed as one who says: *Nunc dimittis Servum tuum, Domine, secundum verbum tuum in pace: quia viderunt oculi mei*—elsewhere or earlier—*salutare tuum*. The minstrels and romancers knew little enough of these mysteries, for the most part, and on the basis of the rumours of the book they superposed what they had heard otherwise—the legend of Joseph, the cultus of the Precious Blood, clouds of fables, multiples of relics, *hoc genus omne*. But it is to be noted in fine that the withdrawal into deeper concealment referred more especially to the company as a hidden school, which would be sought and not found, unless God led the quester. And perhaps those who came into contact by accident did not always ask the question: Who administers the Mysteries? Yet, if they were elected they were brought in subsequently.

It will be observed that in this speculation the existence of the rumours which were incorporated does not in a strict sense involve the existence of any book to account for their comparative prevalence.

VII

THE DECLARED MYSTERY OF QUEST

There follow in this place certain exotics of the subject which are not put forward as an integral part thereof, but are offered to those only who are concerned in the rumour of the Graal literature—as expressed in this book—so far as it incorporates that literature in the annals of Christian sanctity. They will know that the sins and imperfections of this our human life are attenuated by the turning of our intellectual part towards the Blessed Zion, and that, next after leading the all-hallowed life, the making of holy books to formulate the aspirations of our best part in its best moments is counted in a man towards righteousness. It is well, indeed, for him whose life is dedicated to the Quest, but at least—in the stress and terror of these our wayward times—in the heart and the inmost heart let us keep its memory green.

1. Faith is the implicits of the mind passing into expression formally, and knowledge is the same implicits certified by experience. It is in this sense that

The Hidden Church of the Holy Graal

God recompenses those who seek Him out. The Mystery of the Holy Graal is the sun of a great implicit rising in the zones of consciousness.

2. If, therefore, from one point of view we are dealing with great speculations, from another we are truly concerned with great certainties; and Galahad did not question or falter.

3. There is nothing in the world which has less to do with a process or other conventions and artifices than the ascent of a soul to light. Thus, the Quest had no formulæ.

4. The mistake which man has made has been to go in search of his soul, which does not need finding but entering only, and that by a certain door which is always open within him. All the doors of Corbenic were open when Lancelot came thereto, even that sanctuary into which he could look from afar but wherein he could not enter. The chief door is inscribed: *Sapida notitia de Deo.*

5. It is understood, however, that before the door is reached there are gates which are well guarded. So on a night at midnight, when the moon shone clear, Lancelot paused at the postern, which opened toward the sea, and saw how two lions guarded the entrance.

6. It is true also that the gates are not opened easily by which the King of Glory comes in; yet we know that the King comes. The key of these gates is called *Voluntas inflammata.* This will works on the hither side, but there is another which works on the further, and this is named *Beneplacitum termino carens.* When the gates open by the concurrence of the two powers, the King of Salem comes forth carrying Bread and Wine. Of the communication which then follows it is said: *Gustari potest quod explicari nequit.* Galahad and his fellows did taste and saw that the Lord is sweet.

7. For the proselytes of the gate which is external and the postulants at the pronaos of the temple, the Crucifixion took place on Calvary. For the adepts and the

epopts, the question, if it can be said to arise, is not whether this is true on the plane of history, but in what manner it signifies, seeing that the great event of all human history began at the foundation of the world, as it still takes place daily in the soul of every man for whom the one thing needful is to know when Christ shall arise within him. It is then that those on the Quest can say with Sir Bors: "But God was ever my comfort."

8. All that we forget is immaterial if that which we remember is vital, as, for example, the Lord of Quest, who said: "Therefore I wote wel whan my body is dede, my sowle shalle be in grete joye to see the blessid Trynyte every day, and the mageste of oure lord Jhesu Cryst"—in other words, *Contemplatio perfectissima et altissima Dei*.

9. The first condition of interior progress is in detachment from the lesser responsibilities which—because they have not entered into the heart of hearts—are external to our proper interests and distract from those high and onerous burdens which we have to carry on our road upward, until such time as even the road itself—and the burdens thereto belonging—shall assume and transport us. From the greatest even to the least the missions of knight-errantry were followed in utter detachment, and those who went on the Quest carried no *impedimenta*. So also is the great silence ordained about those who would hear the *interior Dei locutio altissimi*.

10. The generation of God is outward and so into the estate of man; but the generation of man—which is called also rebirth—is inward, and so into the Divine Union. The great clerks wrote the adventures of the Graal in great books, but there was no rehearsal of the last branch, the first rubric of which would read: *De felicissima animæ cum Deo unione*.

11. Most conventions of man concern questions of procedure, and it is so with the things which are above, for we must either proceed or perish. Sir Gawain turned back, and hence he was smitten of the old wound

that Lancelot gave him; but no knight who achieved the Quest died in arms, unless in Holy War.

12. In the declared knowledge which behind it has the hidden knowledge, blood is the symbol of life, and this being so it can be understood after what manner the Precious Blood profiteth and the Reliquary thereof. The other name of this Reliquary is Holy Church. But such are the offices of its mercy that *in examine mortis* even Gawain received his Saviour.

13. The root from which springs the great tree of mysticism is the old theological doctrine that God is the centre of the heart. He is by alternative the soul's centre. This is the ground of the union: *per charitatem justi uniuntur cum Deo.* Gawain entreated Lancelot to "praye some prayer more or lesse for my soule;" King Arthur as he drifted in the dark barge said to Bedivere: "And yf thou here neuer more of me praye for my soule," but Perceval and Galahad knew that their reward was with them; they asked for no offerings and no one wearied Heaven.

14. In the soul's conversion there is no office of time, and this is why the greatest changes are always out of expectation. The Graal came like angels—unawares. The *castissimus et purissimus amplexus* and the *felix osculum* are given as in the dark and suddenly. There is further nothing in the wide world so swift and so silent as the *illapsus Christi in centrum animæ.* So also it is said of Galahad that "sodenely his soule departed."

15. The five changes of the Graal are analogous to the five natures of man, and these in their turn correspond to the four aspects of the cosmos and that which rules all things within and from above the cosmos.

16. The consideration of eternity arises from that of the Holy Graal, as from all literature at its highest, and if I have set it as the term of my own researches, in this respect, it is rather because it has imposed itself than because I have sought it out.

Mystic Aspects of the Graal Legend

Obiter Dicta.

And now as the sum total of these mystical aspects, the desire of the eyes in the seeking and finding of the Holy Graal may, I think, be re-expressed as follows:—

Temple or Palace or Castle—Mont Salvatch or Corbenic—wherever located and whether described as a wilderness of building, crowded burg or simple hermit's hold—there is one characteristic concerning the sanctuary which, amidst all its variations in the accidents, is essentially the same; the Keeper of the great Hallows has fallen upon evil days; the means of restoration and of healing are, as one would say, all around him, yet the help must come from without; it is that of his predestined successor, whose office is to remove the vessel, so that it is henceforth never seen so openly. Taking the Quest of Galahad as that which has the highest significance spiritually, I think that we may speak of it thus:—We know that in the last analysis it is the inward man who is really the Wounded Keeper. The mysteries are his; on him the woe has fallen; it is he who expects healing and redemption. His body is the Graal Castle, which is also the castle of Souls, and behind it is the Earthly Paradise as a vague and latent memory. We may not be able to translate the matter of the romance entirely into mystical symbolism, since it is only a rumour at a distance of life in the spirit and its great secrets. But, I think, we can see that it all works together for the one end of all. He who enters into the consideration of this secret and immemorial house under fitting guidance shall know why it is that the Graal is served by a pure maiden, and why that maiden is ultimately dispossessed. Helayne is the soul, and the soul is in exile because all the high unions have been declared voided—the crown has been separated from the kingdom, and experience from the higher knowledge. So long as she remained a pure virgin, she was more than a thyrsus bearer in the mysteries, but the morganatic marriage of mortal life is part of her doom. This is still a high destiny, for the soul out of earthly experience brings forth spiritual desire, which is the quest of the return journey, and this is Galahad. It is therefore within the law and the order that she has to conceive and bring him forth. Galahad represents the highest spiritual aspirations and desires passing into full consciousness, and so into attainment. But he is not reared by his mother, because Eros, which is the higher knowledge, has dedicated the true desire to the proper ends thereof. It will be seen also what must be understood by Lancelot in secret communication with Helayne, though he has taken her throughout for another. The reason is that it is impossible to marry even in hell without marrying that seed which is of heaven. As she is the psychic woman, so is he the natural man, or rather the natural intelligence which is not without its consecrations, not without its term in the highest. Helayne believes that her desire is only for Lancelot, but this is because she takes him for Eros, and it is by such a misconception that the lesser Heaven stoops to the earth; herein also there is a sacred dispensation, because so is the earth assumed. I have said that Lancelot is the natural man, but he is such merely at the highest; he is born in great sorrow, and she who has conceived him saves her soul alive amidst the offices of external religion. He is carried into the lesser land of Faerie, as into a garden of childhood. When he draws towards manhood, he comes forth from the first places of enchantment and is clothed upon by the active duties of life as by the vestures of chivalry. He enters also into the unsanctified life of sense, into an union against the consecrated life and order. But his redeeming quality is that he is faithful and true, because of which, and because of his genealogy, he is chosen to beget Galahad, of whom he is otherwise unworthy, even as we all, in our daily life, fall short of the higher aspirations of the soul. As regards the Keeper, it is certain that he must die and be replaced by

Mystic Aspects of the Graal Legend

another Keeper before the true man can be raised, with the holy things to him belonging, which Hallows are indeed withdrawn, but it is with and in respect of him only, for the keepers are a great multitude, though it is certain that the Graal is one. The path of quest is the path of upward progress, and it is only at the great height that Galahad knows himself as really the Wounded Keeper and that thus, in the last resource, the physician heals himself. Now this is the mystery from everlasting, which is called in the high doctrine *Schema misericordiæ*. It is said: *Latet, æternumque latebit*, until it is revealed in us; and as to this: *Te rogamus, audi nos*.

This is the end of this publication.

Any remaining blank pages are for our book binding requirements and are blank on purpose.

To search thousands of interesting publications like this one, please remember to visit our website at:

http://www.kessinger.net

CPSIA information can be obtained
at www.ICGtesting.com
Printed in the USA
LVHW061447100919
630590LV00010B/311/P